Spirit of the Living Room

Spirit of the Living Room

Jane Alexander

WATSON-GUPTILL PUBLICATIONS/NEW YORK

First published in the United States in 2002 by
Watson-Guptill Publications
a division of VNU Business Media, Inc.
770 Broadway, New York, New York 10003
www.watsonguptill.com

First published in the UK in 2002 by Element
An imprint of HarperCollins*Publishers*
77-85 Fulham Palace Road
Hammersmith, London W6 8JB

1 2 3 4 5 6 / 07 06 05 04 03 02

Jane Alexander asserts the moral right
to be identified as the author of this work
Editor: Jillian Stewart
Design: Wheelhouse Creative
Production: Melanie Vandevelde

Library of Congress Control Number: 2002102105

ISBN: 0 8230 4904 3

Printed and bound in Hong Kong

Contents

Introduction 1

What is a Living Room? 5

What do you need from your Living Room? 15

The Energetic Living Room 25

Feng Shui Basics... 35

A Friendly, Feel-Good Living Room 45

Stimulate your Senses 55

The Creative Living Room 67

A Room with Spirit.. 80

Resources 89

Introduction

Of all the rooms in the home, the living room is probably the most complex. Its functions are many and, over the years, its titles and roles have shifted more than most other rooms. Just think about some of the past and present names for this room: drawing room, sitting room, reception room, parlor, lounge, and morning room—to mention just a few. For some families it is the playroom or the family room. Over the last fifty years its roles have become mixed and often confused, so this can be a tricky room. In the course of this little book, we're going to try to untangle what we mean by a living room and what we want from our own.

In the past, most houses had a formal living room. In grand houses, there would be more than one, in fact there would be a host of rooms set aside for various functions: sitting and talking, reading and writing, performing and listening to music, playing games and cards, receiving guests for morning coffee or afternoon tea, "withdrawing" after dinner (the origin of "drawing" rooms), holding parties and dances. In smaller houses, there was precious little time for rest and relaxation so the kitchen would usually provide the stage for everyday family living while a more formal "parlor" would be kept spick and span for visiting guests. Social relations were more formalized, and custom dictated that you needed a place to take your visitors, away from the hurly-burly of everyday life and mess.

Nowadays we may be less formal, but the modern living room still has a wide role to fill. It needs to be a place everyone living in the house can use for rest, relaxation, and play. Yet it also has to provide a welcoming space for visitors to our homes. It should be a warm, enclosing place for when you want to be alone with your thoughts, yet also transform itself into a supreme party place for larger gatherings. The living room—often called the family room these days—is usually the room in which we gather to watch television, to read, to talk,

to entertain ourselves and our friends and family. For many people it is also the room in which they eat (either at a table or in front of the television) and often it is the room in which they work, do homework, and indulge in hobbies. In small apartments and studios, it has to double as sleeping space too. It's a tough job, and no wonder many of us feel perplexed when it comes to making our living rooms work on all these various levels.

Many people would claim the living room is the most important room in the house; yet many of us feel uncomfortable in our living spaces. I think the problem is that we are often caught up in confusion over the role of the living room—and that is something we will discuss (and hopefully overcome) in the chapters that follow.

When I analyze what I like about my own living room it comes down to the fact that it is eminently adaptable. When I close the curtains and light up the bank of candles around the room, it becomes a

cozy retreat. When we fling open the doors and windows, it welcomes in the outside world. By shifting the seating, we can close ourselves in as a family or, by spreading it all out, provide an expansive welcome for friends.

I believe a living room should be a fun place, a soothing space, a room which can shift to become the background for the various aspects of your life. Above all, it needs to reflect your personality, to be a comfortable and friendly room that suits your soul. I'm lucky in that my room is quite large but I hope you will realize, as you read this book, that size is not actually the most important factor. Any room can—with a little thought and imagination—be turned into a nurturing retreat for the solitary soul and also a welcoming space for larger gatherings. It doesn't take vast funds or interior design expertise; sometimes the most effective changes are incredibly cheap or even free. Let's take a look and see what we can do.

What is a Living Room?

What is a living room? Let's start by turning this question around. Instead of asking "What is a living room?" let's think about living rooms that don't work, which aren't spaces for living. On the whole, these tend to be stiff, stylized, highly formal rooms. They are the kind of places in which the very air feels stultified and still. Everything is immaculate, to be sure, but nothing feels very relaxed and comfortable. You perch on the pristine couch or chair and feel the urge to inspect your shoes to make sure you're not going to leave muddy marks on the spotless carpet. In the old-fashioned version of this room the tables are dainty, the ornaments delicate. An alternative is the room stuffed with precious antiques and elaborate drapes. The more modern version is usually a paean to minimalism, with acres of cool cream and white. Whatever its incarnation, even the most careful visitor feels nervous about spilling a cup of coffee or dropping crumbs. If you have children or a dog, your nerves will be at screaming pitch in such a room.

Maybe I have a built-in prejudice (born of numerous childhood visits to the homes of stuffy aunts), but to me these rooms are not living spaces. They are remnants from the past, when polite society dictated that we had a formal receiving room in which to entertain (and impress) our guests. Many of us still cling to this idea. How often have you been ushered into a spotless living room when you'd rather be chatting with your hosts in the kitchen? How often have you shunted your guests into the living room, only to find they refuse to stay put and drift out into messier parts of the house? Why is this?

I think the key lies back in history. When important guests came to the house, they needed to be impressed. It's easy to forget, in our increasingly informal and classless society, how rigid the rules of society and manners were for our not-so-distant forebears. Most social occasions were also, in effect, business meetings. A house, and particularly the formal room, was an indicator of people's prestige, their wealth, their social standing. It was designed to impress; to project an image of class and abundance. It's interesting to note how many of us still cling to the trappings of those rooms: the elaborate drapes, the ornate chandeliers, the ornaments and fancy flower arrangements (even if scaled down to fit our smaller rooms).

In fact, if we're honest with ourselves, this element still prevails. We still "bring the boss" for dinner and try desperately to impress. We still invite our neighbors around and can't quite get rid of that "keeping up with the Joneses" attitude. Blame it on the goddess Hera.

The gods in the living room

While Hestia, goddess of the home and hearth, is the quiet, welcoming presence which makes us feel "at home," Hera's influence is very different. Hera, Queen of the Gods, and goddess of marriage, often holds sway in the living room. In her positive role, she embodies abundance, harmony, community, and closely bonded relationships.

However, Hera also has a strongly negative side which shows itself as jealous, vengeful, and obsessed with power, prestige, and rectitude. Psychologically, she has been portrayed as the "career wife," the woman who will do anything to "get her man" and will go to any stakes to keep his position assured (Lady Macbeth could be seen as an extreme example). Over the years this archetype has been ridiculed, and women who show a marked Hera aspect to their characters have been scorned and reviled.

Yet a swift look at Hera's history gives some clues to her ambivalence and may give us some ideas about how to pacify her—in ourselves and in our homes. Originally Hera was worshiped as an aspect of the great Mother Goddess, the supreme nurturer. An ancient myth says that when milk spurted from Hera's breasts, the drops that fell to earth became lilies, while those that flew into the sky transformed into the Milky Way. The name Hera is thought to mean "Great Lady" and is the feminine form of the Greek word *hero*. She was a goddess of great power but also a source of nourishment and comfort. With the rise of a more androcentric religion, Hera was demoted. She became the consort of Zeus, the great Father god, but sadly her role diminished to that of supportive wife. Yet Hera never gave in. As if demonstrating the inequality of her position, she constantly undermined Zeus and jealously attacked his many mistresses.

Hera is a strongly protective presence and will guard her family like a she-bear will guard its cubs. She revels in a closely knit family and mutually honoring relationships. A statue of Hera or one of the mother goddesses will guard your living room and keep watch (she is also associated with watchfulness). You could also encourage the positive aspects of her influence with the following:

- Spend the odd evening actually talking to your partner, rather than slumping in front of the television. Light a fire, crack open a bottle of wine, remember what it was like when you first met.
- Choose furniture and fabrics together—even if it's just making that final decision as a unit.

- Have family get-togethers as often as possible—talk, play games, make music together. It may feel stilted at first if you're used to going your separate ways or sitting in silence watching TV—but persevere.
- Make your living room beautiful— Hera is associated with lilies, so honor her with a vase of them (the scent is lovely too). Plant them outside the window so the scent wafts in.
- The peacock's stunning feathers are a symbol of Hera, so think about subtly introducing this pattern, or their iridescent sheen, to fabrics and accessories.
- The cow is also a symbol of Hera— display an image of the sacred cow or Hathor, the Egyptian counterpart to Hera. Other images include a winged goddess (as Isis) or the goddess embracing a golden eagle.

- Hera is associated with the number three, so indulge her with trinities (for instance, mother, father, child; Maiden, Mother, Crone). Honor her with groupings of three—three candles, three photograph frames, three beautiful stones, etc.

Honor Hera and she will be a benign and gently watchful presence in your living room. However, ignore her or incite her wrath and she transforms into a steely, cold, ruthless character. Hera can be the force that makes you turn your living room into a room devoid of character and warmth; into a room devoted to image and power, prestige and vanity. Her love of marriage and family can tilt into a rigid requirement for rules and responsibility, for tradition above all else. She is the force that turns what should be welcoming gatherings into tense, uncomfortable ordeals.

The antidote to this lies (interestingly enough) with Zeus, Hera's unfaithful partner and father of the Gods. Whatever we may think about Zeus, he does have some good points. Yes, he's egocentric, vain, and a terminal womanizer, but he is also endlessly creative, wildly imaginative, and spontaneous. Zeus loves beauty and magic, and craves self-expression. Put Zeus and Hera together and you have the perfect marriage; they represent two facets of the human psyche, mutually dependent yet always testing each other. Whenever you feel that Hera is about to overwhelm you (a too-rigid prescription for a dinner party perhaps or an overly regal window treatment?), invoke a little Zeus-like wildness and imagination into the equation to loosen it all up a bit.

Of course, other archetypes sneak into our living rooms. Anthony Lawlor, author of *A Home for the Soul*, believes the living

room is also the abode of Hermes, the messenger god. "Since ancient times, people have drawn together to exchange news, gossip, knowledge, and insight," he says. "Hunters related their exploits, farmers shared know-how, shamans explained the creation of the world and the activities of the gods, families shared the happenings of the day." Hermes, however, can be a trickster god and one we need to watch with caution. He certainly governs conversation, gossip, and lively exchanges but the television is also his toy. While I'm not remotely suggesting you give up television (I'm certainly not prepared to), it's worth keeping an eye on whether you use TV or whether it governs you. If you routinely keep the television on all evening (or even all day), regardless of what is on; if you regularly channel-hop; if you eat all your meals glued to the box, it's time to put Hermes back in his place, as he is beguiling you.

What do you need from your Living Room?

Before you pick up a paintbrush or even ponder color schemes, let's spend some time figuring out the roles you require from your living room.

The technique we're going to try first illustrates how the room is used by each member of the family. Every member of the household takes a sheet of paper on which you have drawn a plan of the room. It need not be draftsman quality but should be roughly to scale with all the major pieces of furniture sketched in.

Now choose a color for each member of the household. Then each of you colors in the room according to who uses each part of it the most. So, for example, if a certain chair "belongs" to X, color it in "their" color. If two or three of you share the table, you may want to use stripes or some other code. Think about who uses each area most and color it correspondingly. This exercise sounds almost facile but it can be very telling. A living room needs to work for everyone in the home, yet many of us are unconsciously colonizing parts of ours—or allowing our rooms to be overrun. After you complete this exercise, sit down and look at your plans. Do you all agree on them? Use the plans as the starting point for a discussion on how the space could be better—or more fairly—used.

Many living rooms are used almost on a time-share basis. Some people use the living room at one time of day, then others take over. Often problems can ensue when the trappings of one role remain when other roles need to take over. I found this when I had my young son, James. During the day we would play in the living room, his toys scattered over the carpet, sofa, and table. Come evening and James's bedtime, my husband and I were tripping over blocks and balls. Even when we tidied them away, the room was in danger of becoming taken over; it was

a playroom over and above any other role. The solution was surprisingly simple. At the end of the day, toys were all put away (with James helping) and stashed in another room. We were then able to reclaim the living room as "adult" space for the evening. If you don't have an extra room, you can achieve the same effect with clever storage. A row of low cabinets or a sideboard looks fashionable yet provides out-of-sight storage for toys—or indeed other needs (such as work paraphernalia if your living room doubles as work space). There are coffee tables that resemble large chests—lift the lid and there is another hidden space for storage.

If you live on your own you can be free and easy with your clutter, but large families or groups sharing need to be sensitive to the needs of other housemates—whatever their age. You could, perhaps, use this opportunity to agree on terms. For instance, once homework is done, all books are packed away. In return, adults could undertake not to spread their own detritus around during play and homework time.

What kind of room do you want?

Once you've ascertained how you already use your room—and maybe come up with some ideas on how to use it better—you can move on to investigating the feel you want from your room. This is where the good old "treasure map" proves invaluable. I've described this in many of my previous books, but in case you haven't read any, I'll briefly recap. A treasure map is a kind of wake-up call to the psyche—it is a way of talking to your unconscious mind and it can be

incredibly powerful. If you worry that you will end up with a particular kind of living room because it's "fashionable" or "trendy" or simply because you have no idea of what style you like, this is certainly for you. We all have wildly different likes, needs, and wants and sometimes it can be hard to see the wood for the trees. I'm painfully aware that my choice of design is not for everyone and that what I love you might abhor—and vice versa. The treasure map

is a really neat way of figuring out exactly what you really want—way down beneath all the expectations and fashion dictates.

All you have to do is to look out for images that really speak to your soul. These may be pictures of your "perfect" living room, cut out of homes magazines. Or they could be more abstract lifestyle shots, such as people doing yoga, or children playing, or a bird singing, or a sunrise... whatever. Equally, you may feel moved by a particular

painting, or postcard, or symbol, or sign, or color. The images need to spark a real reaction in you—that kind of solar plexus "oof" feeling in the gut or a warm fuzzy feeling in the heart (you will know when you see them). Cut them out and stick them on a large sheet of paper. Add photographs of yourself and the other people who share your space. Now put the map where you will see it every day. You may find that, as the days pass, some images don't feel right anymore.

Take them down and replace them with others if you feel so moved.

Once you have lived with your treasure map for a few weeks (do give it that long), you will probably find you have a much better idea of what you want from your living room. It may be as precise as a particular flooring or fabric. It may be far more subtle than that: a sense of the mood or ambience you want in the room. Use it as a springboard for your planning. You may find something even more magical happens. When you give your unconscious mind images, it often finds extraordinary ways of bringing those things into your life. You may just find that someone, out of the blue, offers you a reclaimed wood table similar to the one in your map. Or you notice an ad for a student offering to sand floors for an incredibly reasonable rate. Or a friend comes back from India and unrolls a treasure trove of jewel-like sari fabric. Trust me, these things do happen.

Shifting roles

Of all the rooms in the house, the living room is the most likely to need to shift and change in order to fulfill its various roles. You may find when you look at your treasure map that you want at least three rooms (if not more) all rolled into one.

First of all, stop and think how often you require it to play host to each role. Draw a circle on a piece of paper (upend a medium-sized mixing bowl and draw around it to get a good size). Now make a list of all the roles your living room carries out (or you would like it to carry out). For example, you might include playroom; meditation space; yoga studio; solo comfort zone (for reading, thinking, watching TV); café (for friendly chats with neighbors and friends); artist's studio; study (for paying bills, writing letters); party zone; family den. Now divide your circle into segments for each activity. The size of each segment will depend on how much time is devoted to that activity. Once you've done this you may be surprised how one role overtakes all the rest. Is that appropriate? Possibly, but not necessarily. Should you carve out a little more time for some of the other activities? Think about getting the best possible balance among all your needs. Once again, it can be interesting to get the other household members to do this (their versions may be wildly different from yours).

This balance of activities may help you in deciding on your décor. Is it really appropriate to get your living room done out as a pure white meditation space if you actually carry out most of your meditation in your bedroom and use your living room for lively get-togethers?

Is there much point in stuffing your room with a large table and chairs if you barely entertain (in which case you could think about an expanding table and folding chairs that can be stashed away most of the time)? A living room should be appropriate to the activities carried out in it.

Your "type" of living room

Another way of looking at how to design your living room is to work with your personality type. It's a fact of life that, however much you might adore the look of sleek minimalism, unless you are a certain type of person, you will never ever achieve it. With all the goodwill in the world, the clutter and ornaments will creep back in. Equally, some people will never be at home with wild prints and eccentric furniture—they like things sensible and functional. According to the

psychologist Carl Jung, that is because we all fall into four distinct types—Thinking, Feeling, Sensation, and Intuition types. Each of us will tend to be a mixture of perhaps two or three of these types—though one can often dominate. If you have a strong thinking function, you probably barely notice your surroundings and aren't really interested in fads and fashions—as long as you have somewhere to put your books (or whatever interests you) you'll be happy. The feeling type is virtually the opposite. This type has very strong responses to everything in the home: furnishings, design, color, tone. They therefore tend to go to a lot of trouble to design a beautiful home. People who have a strong sensation function are concerned, above all, with things working well—the home of a sensation type will run like clockwork. Intuitives, on the other hand,

are highly sensitive to atmosphere and are not concerned with practicalities. They can be the most original of all the types when it comes to creating an unusual and individual home. If you are interested in these ideas, they are covered in more detail in *Spirit of the Home* (see "Further Reading" section).

A book I very much like, which follows a similar vein, is *The Domain Book of Intuitive Home Design* by Judy George and Todd Lyon (Potter). This also divides people into four categories—Visionaries (who crave beauty rooted in tradition); Artisans (who desire softness, comfort, and joy); Idealists (who tend to modern, minimalist structures, and spaces); and Adventurers (who indulge in the senses and adore drama, fun, and frolic in their homes). The two systems overlap and can both provide food for thought when plotting your room scheme.

The Energetic Living Room

Even now, we're not ready to tackle the nuts and bolts, curtains and carpets, of your room. We need to look at something far more basic—energy. Energy working is the one practice that you never see on all those home improvement TV shows—yet it can make as much difference as a coat of fresh paint (and often far more).

Ancient philosophy and modern science both teach that our world is not merely material, it is also energetic. Everything we see, be it a person, a dog, a table, a stone, is actually an energy structure that constantly shifts and changes. We may experience our environment as physical, stable, corporeal—but its essence is a shimmering web of energy. Once you take this idea on board (which can be tricky), it begins to make sense that you can alter, mend, and heal the unseen atmosphere of a space. Methods such as space clearing, smudging, and feng shui (and its Indian counterpart Vastu Shastra) have been used for millennia. In the West we have tended to forget them (although vestiges remain in the use of

incense and bells in churches and temples) and think that all we need do to clean a space is to wash the floor and dust the furniture. However, before we look at a few of these somewhat esoteric practices, we need to do something far more down-to-earth.

Decluttering

As you are probably aware, clutter is an absolute disaster energy-wise. If a room (or desk) is filled with clutter and detritus, it will affect you physically (it attracts dust, which may trigger allergies), psychologically (your mind will feel muddled and you'll find it tough to concentrate and focus), and also spiritually (when clutter accumulates in your space, energy can't move freely and you will find yourself blocked in many ways). As you can imagine, the living room above all other rooms is prone to clutter, so be very aware and try to fight it

  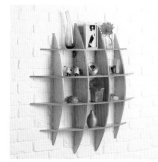

all you can. This isn't a call for pristine minimalism (unless that's your thing) but it is a plea for regular clearing and decluttering.

Spend time sorting out your stuff. Do you like everything in your room? If not, maybe it's time to give it away, sell it, or pass it on? If you have a desk, check the drawers and throw away anything that's no longer needed. Is your magazine rack bulging? Scan the mags for pictures for your treasure map and then recycle. Books you'll never read again? Give them to charity. Old CDs and tapes? Ditto. Are you storing up old letters and photos when they harbor painful memories? Have a ritual and burn them. Store happy photos in albums and put the most important letters in a beautifully covered box. However, do make sure you're not wallowing in the past—if so, try taking Clematis and Walnut Bach Flower remedies. If other people's stuff is your problem give them fair warning that you are clearing out and, if their things aren't removed by a certain date or hour, they will be donated to charity. Be polite but firm—it's really not your problem.

If you need more help on the clutter question *Spirit of the Home* is useful (see "Further Reading"). *Clear Your Clutter with Feng Shui* by Karen Kingston is also inspirational. Once you've cleared your space, clean it thoroughly using nontoxic cleaning materials. Then you will be ready for space clearing.

Space clearing

Space clearing is a vital process, particularly in rooms that experience a lot of emotional "stuff." Over the years the standard living room will witness a host of scenes—from intense joy to utter sorrow; from warmth and gentleness to bitter rows and recriminations. These emotions tend to stick to the walls like psychic glue. Imagine you hadn't physically cleaned your living room in a year. It would be pretty grimy. Yet few houses are ever space cleansed and the psychic "gunk" can get really thick and unpleasant. Still skeptical? Who hasn't walked into a room and felt you could "cut the air with a knife"? Who hasn't found themselves saying, "This room

has such a lovely atmosphere" or "I feel uneasy in that room, but I don't know why"? If you want to shift the energy of your living room, you need to do some cleansing. The process is actually quite easy.

Preparing for space clearing

Although space clearing is generally totally safe, there are several guidelines you should follow before clearing your home.

- Don't perform space clearing if you feel scared or apprehensive. If you feel a room has any kind of evil presence then you should seek out a trained professional (contact your local church or psychic center). Most of the energy in homes is just stuck or stale but some places do seem to have something heavier—call it a ghost,

spirit, whatever—and you shouldn't try to shift that by yourself.

- Choose a time for space clearing when you feel fit, healthy, and emotionally balanced. Don't perform space clearing if you are pregnant or menstruating, as these are times when your energy should be turned within rather than without.
- Before you space clear, ensure you have carried out all your de-cluttering and have given the room a good physical spring cleaning.
- Spend time thinking about what you want to achieve with your space clearing. Look back at your treasure map and try to encapsulate your desires into one or two sentences of clear intent such as "My living room offers joy, fun, and a warm welcome to all" or "My living room nurtures and comforts me—it is a healing, gentle place." Something along these lines is fine.
- Before you start work, have a shower or a bath (you could use a few drops of a purifying oil such as lavender, juniper, or rosemary), wash your hair, and brush your teeth. Put on clean, fresh comfortable clothes. Remove any jewelry, don't put your watch back on and avoid metal belts and buckles.
- If the weather is warm, it's best to be barefoot for space clearing. However, if you're space clearing in a cold house, then wear cotton socks or leather-soled slippers.

Space-clearing ritual

1 Take some time first of all to center yourself. Breathe deeply and evenly and allow yourself to feel calm and balanced. Visualize yourself surrounded by your aura, an egg-shaped cocoon filled with soft white light. Now expand that light to fill the whole of your living room. If it feels more natural, you can choose another color—perhaps pure blue light, a soft rosy pink, gold, or golden pink.

2 Now, starting at the main entrance to your room, hold your hand a few inches away from the wall and start to "sense" the energy. You should find, after a little practice, that this comes quite easily. Your palm should face toward the wall, with your hand roughly parallel with your shoulder. The motion is similar to stroking a cat. You may find as you do this that you begin to

get impressions. Work around your room in this way, picking up feelings, sensing for "dull" or "stuck" spots where the energy feels sluggish or thick. These will need most attention later.

3 Clapping. The basic move of space clearing is clapping. Move steadily around the room systematically clapping into every corner, nook, and cranny. It sounds so simple but this is all it takes: you clap your hands into the corner, starting low and swiftly clapping on up toward the ceiling as high as you can. Repeat this as many times as necessary. You will know when you've clapped the corner clear because the sound of your clapping will become clearer. If you're still not sure, check the energy of the corner with your outstretched hand. As you clap

imagine your clapping is dispersing all the stagnant energy. Follow this procedure around your whole space.

4 When you have finished your clapping, wash your hands thoroughly under running water.

5 Most professional space clearers would now use a bell. If you have a bell with a really pure, clear tone, use that. Simply walk around the room again, this time ringing the bell as you go along. Your aim is to create a continuous circle of sound, so you need to ring the bell again before the last tone has died away. When you get back to your starting point, draw a horizontal figure eight in the air with your bell. If you don't have a bell, don't worry—you will have done some serious cleansing with your clapping alone.

6 You may also like to use a space-clearing spray. Despite their names, I find they work best when combined with traditional space-clearing methods described above. They leave a lovely scent and can add an extra dimension to the work. For the living room I would recommend Space Clearing essence mist by Australian Bush Flower Essences, Purification by Alaskan Flower Essences, or Heart Spirit by Pacific Essences (see "Resources").

7 Finally, you need to seal your newly energized and clean room. Fill the space once again with your expanded aura, imagining any remaining stagnant energy being pushed clean out of the room. Now you should shield the space. Stand at each corner of your room and imagine yourself bringing down a force-field of energy with a downward sweep of your arm. The four fields merge together and create a safe haven, protecting you and your space.

Feng Shui Basics

Having enjoyed huge popularity over the last decade, feng shui is probably no longer "the thing" in fashionable circles. But don't be put off by the ebb and flow of fashion and design. Feng shui, the Chinese art and science of placement, can make a huge and noticeable difference to your space.

Feng shui works rather like acupuncture for houses. The ancient Chinese noticed that certain kinds of energy could be attracted or repelled by particular ways of siting buildings, rooms, and the objects within them. Out of this grew an entire science based on centuries of careful observation and practice. Despite this, many people are still skeptical. My advice would be to try it out. Many of the suggestions are pure common sense, and both simple and cost-free to perform. See for yourself if it works. In my experience, it invariably does. I was actually very skeptical myself on first hearing about feng shui but agreed to make changes to improve my (then failing) finances. To be honest, I thought I would be able to gloatingly report that it was a load of bunkum.

To my huge surprise and unending gratitude I was offered (out of the blue) a job which quadrupled my income overnight. Coincidence? Who cares—from then on, I have always used feng shui in my homes and offices.

The ba-gua

At the heart of feng shui lies the ba-gua. This is an octagonal template that divides any space—your entire home or simply a room within it—into eight areas. These eight areas, or corners, represent Wealth (finances in general), Fame (how you appear to the outside world), Marriage (and all close relationships), Children (and any other creative process), Helpful People, Career (your path through life), Knowledge (wisdom, inner knowing, spirituality), and The Family (including your ancestors).

The Ba-gua

Different practitioners of feng shui use the ba-gua in different ways. However, all the feng shui consultants I have met so far use this format which is, to my mind, also the most straightforward to learn. If you already know a fair amount about feng shui and use another method, stick with that by all means.

To work out the ba-gua of any room or house, the position of the main door is important. Imagine yourself looking into your home or living room, standing with your back to the door. Depending on the position of the main door, you will be standing in either the Knowledge, Career, or Helpful People corner of the ba-gua. Now envisage the ba-gua laid over your space. The Wealth corner will be off in the far-lefthand corner, the Marriage corner in the far-righthand corner. You may find it easier to draw a map of your home and sketch the ba-gua over it, giving you an immediate idea of which corner lies in which room. Obviously, the task is easy if your house is square, but you can apply the ba-gua to any building or room, as illustrated here.

First of all, map your entire apartment or house. In which area does your living room fall? Inevitably, the energy of that segment of the ba-gua will affect your room. For example:

- A living room in the Marriage, Family, or Helpful People areas of the room will augur a warm and friendly environment. If it falls into Marriage, make sure other people don't feel excluded.

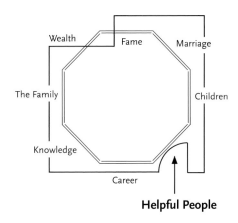

Helpful People

- A living room in the Knowledge area should be a great learning space—but make sure you can let your hair down and have fun there too.
- In the Children (creativity) space you will have lots of fun—but it might not be an ideal spot if your living room needs to double up as a work space (if your work is more methodical than creative).
- Watch out if your living room is in Career—you may find you always bring your work home with you.

- Equally, Fame can be tricky—your space may fall too far into Hera's realm (see the first chapter, "What is a Living Room?") and become a pretentious showroom.
- A living room in the Wealth area is fine (the lively energy is highly beneficial for financial energy), but do make sure you keep it clear of clutter or your finances could suffer.

Now let's apply the ba-gua to the living room itself. Stand on the threshold of the living room with your back to the door. Once again, depending on where the door lies, you will be standing in either the Career area (the center), Helpful People (righthand corner), or Knowledge (lefthand corner)—remember Wealth will lie off in the far-lefthand corner and Marriage in the far-righthand corner. Plot the ba-gua of the living room and use it to decide how you arrange the furniture.

- If you work from your living room (or have a desk on which you do occasional work-related tasks) you might like to have your desk in the Career area to give a boost to your work.
- A telephone could sit in the Helpful People area—and you may discover that finding a decent plumber or a last-minute flower delivery isn't as difficult as usual.
- Knowledge is the perfect spot for a bookcase or for the table on which the children do their homework or you study for your after-hours degree.
- A cozy two-seater in the Marriage area will help couples snuggle up together and keep intimacy alive (rather than sitting in separate "power" chairs).
- Equally, comfortable seating in the Family area will keep a family talking together (or perhaps put your dining room table here if you eat in this room).

Notice if any areas are still cluttered (though hopefully you will have cleared it all by now). If so, which areas are they? A cluttered Wealth area can cause financial difficulties; a cluttered Marriage area, difficulties in close relationships—and so on. If you want to boost a particular area you can do this by placing something symbolic in that space. A bright light will often literally "illuminate" an area. A fishbowl with healthy, happy fish is considered very beneficial (if you don't want fish, try a waterfall or bubbling water feature).

A note on televisions

Televisions (and stereos) are supposed to boost energy in feng shui terms. However, my own feeling is that the television should not dominate the room. In an ideal world I would put the television in a separate room or make sure it can be hidden away in a cupboard to ensure it doesn't rule your life. Nowadays, many homes have a huge television center-stage in the living room where, to my mind, the hearth should be.

When we watch nonstop or indiscriminate television we harm both our health (TVs give out electro-magnetic fields which are injurious to health) and our minds (television has killed many relationships as people forget how to talk to one another). Of course, there are good TV shows, but be discriminating. Children, in particular, can become "square-eyed" very easily, so limit their viewing and, if they are young, encourage them to talk about what they are watching—so they don't descend into a kind of fugue state. Make sure you sit as far as possible away from the set— under no circumstances allow children to sit with their noses virtually pressed against it.

Feng shui expert Sarah Shurety recommends you have a fish tank, or something bright and eye-catching, near the television to draw some of the energy away from it and release people from its tyranny.

Other feng shui tips

- Keep shapes in your living room soft and rounded. This prevents "cutting *qi*" which can cause arguments and irritation. Soft, squashy sofas fit the bill, as do rounded beanbags (which now come in leather, suede, and other sophisticated fabrics) and ottomans.

- Colors should be warm and inviting— try yellow, purple, peach, and pink. If those aren't to your taste, don't panic; we'll look at other possibilities in the next chapter.

- Coffee tables and dining tables ideally should be round or oval to encourage people to come together. If you do crave a square or oblong table try to find one with softened corners—sharp angles send out harmful cutting *qi*.

- If you have shelving in your living room, try to keep it low level as this is less oppressive. This ties in well with the modern fashion for low-level storage and the return of the sideboard.

- Don't stuff your bookshelves full—leave gaps. Not only does this allow you the chance to display interesting objects but also gives the opportunity for fresh knowledge to come into your life.
- The most auspicious spot in the room, feng shui-wise, is the chair or sofa that has a clear view of both doors and windows. It lends a natural authority to the person who sits there, so watch out if you let a child sit there—he or she will tend to become disobedient and sassy.
- If the position of your chair means you can't see the door, try to place something large and secure behind you (i.e., a bookcase, desk, screen, or room divider) so you feel less vulnerable.

- Make sure your lighting is adequate for the various needs of the room. In feng shui terms, chandeliers are good news as they are considered to draw people together and make the conversation sparkle. Some enterprising designers are now doing interesting modern takes on the chandelier.
- Hang multifaceted crystals at your window to bring fire energy into your room. If your living room has a horrible view or is overlooked by a large building, tree, or church, or a road comes directly toward it, hang a Mayan ball (from New Age shops) on a piece of red ribbon in the window to deflect the negative cutting *qi*.

A Friendly, Feel-Good Living Room

Modern living rooms should, above all, be comfortable feel-good places. What is the point of a room that looks great, if you don't feel at home? A living room should be inviting, welcoming, beguiling. But how do you achieve that? I think one of the key factors is to try to engage all your senses. Above all, you need to think beyond how something *looks* to how it *feels*. Let's explore this idea.

Floors

Yes, your living-room floor should look good—that goes without saying. But it should also feel good too. Living rooms work hard and it's one room in the house where we are quite likely to get down on the floor—to play games, to stretch, to do yoga, whatever. So bear that in mind when choosing living-room flooring. Before you make your final choice I'd advise you walk across it in bare feet, and that you lie down on it and roll around a bit. Okay, the showroom salesperson might raise an eyebrow but, hey, you would try out a bed, wouldn't you? Go for it.

I can't tell you what floor covering you need for your space. Much will depend on the climate where you live. If you're in a hot spot, there is nothing more delicious than cool flagstones or marble. If you inhabit a chilly part of the world, that could be your worst nightmare. Check out the difference between smooth polished wood and ceramic tiling. Plunge your toes into a thick, shag-pile carpet; explore the rough hairiness of coir and sisal.

Carpet is very body friendly if you live in moderate or cool climes. We tend to look down on carpet but it's a highly practical, feel-good option. Try to go for the best quality you can afford—100 percent wool is ideal. There are companies now using other materials such as cotton, which can look and feel wonderful too—but they may be less hardwearing.

Natural floorings like coir look wonderful but can be a bit itchy if you go in for floor-rolling sessions. Seagrass is the smoothest of that crew as it has a silky finish. However, be warned that these floorings aren't the toughest in the world and can look quite shabby after a short while if exposed to a lot of rough and tumble. They are also a disaster if you have small children—too rough for little knees and a nightmare to keep clean and free from toddler gunk.

Natural wood makes a great flooring. If your own floorboards are good enough, you can simply sand them and, if you

Walls

wish, apply paint or varnish, or simply wax them (choose nontoxic, natural paints and varnishes). If they are past redemption, or you don't have wooden floors, you can install new ones (recycled wood is wonderful and good for your conscience too). I would strongly recommend that you don't go for laminate flooring—it contains a host of nasty toxins. Warm up a wood floor with rugs—the choice is endless: ethnic kilims, bold, modern geometric patterns, homey rag-rugs (make your own?), sophisticated Persians. Some good friends of mine don't just keep their rugs on the floor but also pin beautiful examples of kilims on their cool, cream walls (they look fabulous). My personal belief is that every fireside deserves a hairy or shaggy rug of some description (fake fur, sheepskin, cowhide, whatever).

Paint or wallpaper? It need not be that simple. We often forget that walls can, and should, feel nice too. Think about the rough, uneven surface of old plaster, the molded contours of wood paneling, the sheer slide of glass, the cool density of stone. Think about the style and age of your home—what suits it? Plain brick can look great, either left nude or painted, and it feels interesting too. Rough-hewn stone gives a grounded, earthy feel but it needs to be in keeping with its home. Wood paneling can completely transform a room. Rich walnut or golden oak tones give a room an embracing, den-like feel; while painted tongue and groove offers a fresh, almost nautical air.

In the past, it was common to cover walls with fabric. This is a great idea, particularly if you like the idea of changing the mood of your room

quite often—or you live in rented accommodation and aren't allowed to re-paint. Obviously, it's an expensive option if you pick heavy furnishing fabrics but you could easily take cheap fabric and either dye it or paint it to your liking. Fix it on rods and you can shift your room as often as you like. If the all-over treatment is a bit much, consider making your own "tapestries" by hanging a gorgeous piece of fabric over one wall, or framing favorite pieces of fabric.

Windows

Curtains are obvious choices for living rooms, as they work so well. They offer privacy and a lot of freedom in design terms. The curtains you choose can set the whole tone of a room, so pick carefully. Think about color (see next chapter) but also about the fabric. Cottons and linens will give a crisp, cool feel to a room while velvet, brushed, and peached fabrics will give a softer, warmer feel. These kind of fabrics will work well with most traditional window "treatments"—they drape well and can be twisted and tucked to your heart's delight. However, many people are now looking at alternative ways of dressing windows and, if you choose a simple, unfussy hanging, your choice of fabric increases dramatically. Tweeds and tartan plaids give a warm Celtic feel to a room. Hide, suede, and leather are expensive yet can feel wonderful and look wildly original. Wool, mohair, and alpaca are glamorous options. Old lace is romantic, while sheer voiles can look cool and minimal. Felt comes in a huge array of colors and can look cute, folklorish, or strikingly modern, depending on how you employ it. Rummage around and experiment with hanging rugs, tablecloths, saris, wall-hangings... the choice is endless.

Although feng shui experts prefer to keep blinds out of the living room, I have to disagree. Yes, some of them can look overly cool and formal but not all. I love wooden slatted blinds that can filter in varying degrees of light. There are also hoards of new blinds on the market—in a wild variety of materials and designs. Explore the possibilities or make your own (most furnishing departments now offer kits).

Furniture

I don't believe in giving prescriptions for furniture—or anything much else, truth to tell. It's all so individual, it would be presumptuous to dictate. However, I do think that every good living room deserves a generous and welcoming sofa of the largest proportions your room can take. Why? Because a massive sofa offers so many possibilities. My own is huge

(because I used to live in a house with huge rooms). When we moved to our new (smaller roomed) house I seriously thought we'd have to change sofas but, not having the spare cash, decided we'd live with it—and I'm glad we did. It will happily accommodate four adults sitting or one (or two friendly ones) stretched right out. It willingly transforms itself into a "jungle" or a "castle" for small children. If extra guests come, it becomes a bed. You'd be surprised how even very small rooms can cope and benefit from large furniture. Just because you have a teeny house or apartment, you don't need to think small and dainty if your soul craves big and wide. Some friends of ours live in a cottage with a minute living room but are the proud owners of an expansive, bright-yellow sofa—and it does the job brilliantly.

Aside from that, I think seating should be flexible. A combination of chairs,

ottomans, and beanbags works well, according to your needs. Daybeds and couches look gorgeous and invite you to curl up with a book and a cup of coffee—or have an after-dinner snooze. A rocking chair in a quiet corner (perhaps by a window with a lovely view) will be a welcome refuge.

Children love their own furniture—and it need not interfere with your design sensibilities. Shun garish plastic and track down beautiful pint-sized chairs and rocking chairs (or commission a local craftsperson to make one). I discovered some gorgeous African three-legged wooden stools—these sit under our coffee table and can be pulled out to seat small visitors. When not in use they double up as stylish candle-holders.

If your living room has to be multifunctional, then screens or room dividers can be very useful. After all, you don't want to be looking at your work desk (and thinking of all your unfinished business) while you're trying to relax. You can buy unfinished screens or "blank" ones, which can be painted or decorated according to your whim. I've even seen wonderful screens capable of housing hoards of photographs; certainly a talking point.

When choosing fabrics for sofas and chairs, use your imagination. Look back at the ideas given for curtains and flex your options. Don't forget to be fairly practical though. There's no point having an upholstered sofa in a delicate cream fabric if you've got small children and dogs—or if you have lots of parties. In such cases, loose covers that can be washed at a reasonably high temperature are best. If you can't afford to buy new furniture, then think about loose covers for your existing stuff. Still too expensive? Invest in some wonderful throws and a panoply of extravagant cushions—they will quite transform a room and need not cost the earth.

Stimulate your Senses

A living room should indulge all your senses. We've already talked a little about the sense of touch, about introducing texture and concentrating on building up a feel-good living room. Now it's time to explore how we can indulge our other senses. Let's start with our vision—and the intriguing world of color.

Sight and color

Never underestimate the power of color. Even if you don't consider yourself a particularly visual person, you will still be affected by the colors with which you surround yourself, because our whole body reacts to color. We don't just "see" color with our eyes, we feel it and sense it as well. Experiments have shown that people can "feel" color with their fingertips when blindfolded. So don't just settle for magnolia—choose your colors with care.

What I love about color is that you can change the mood of a room within an hour or so. Slapping on a fresh coat of paint is quick and relatively cheap. However, we tend to be scared of color and go for safe, tried and trusted pastels

and neutrals. If you feel happy with them and they suit your soul, fine. If not, then dare to be a bit more adventurous. Look back at your treasure map and see which colors predominate. Are you drawn to nature's green or the cool blue of summer skies? Does your soul yearn to dance with the fire spirits, the salamanders, of hot reds and spicy oranges? Do your spirits lift when you breathe in the vibrant yellow of daffodils or the soft hue of dainty primroses? What styles of decorating do you like? Are you drawn to the pale winter tones of Gustavian interiors or the warm vibrant hues of a Provençal farmhouse? Do you love the muted serenity of Shaker style or go wild for the hot pinks and turquoises of a Caribbean hideaway?

Remember, your living room is going to have to handle a lot of situations—it needs to look good both in daylight and at night—so check out your prospective colors in both lights. Sometimes a tone that looks fabulous by candlelight looks tawdry in the cold light of day; a color that looks punchy and vibrant in sunshine, can become quite drab at night. Let's look at the choices offered.

RED: Red can increase your pulse, respiration, and brain activity so it will keep you alert—but it can get tiring if you stay in a powerfully red room for a long time. I steer clear of pure red for an entire living room but often like to use it as an accent color in curtains, on sofas, and in rugs. Alternatively, try it on just one wall, as it gives life and spark to a room and is also cozy and welcoming.

PINK: Pink can look sickly; bland and boring; or punchy, vibrant, and right up to the minute. It all depends on the shade you choose and how you use it. A totally pink living room can be a bit too Barbie, but bright pink accessories teamed with white or green walls can

look stunning. So too can one fuschia or shocking-pink wall. Pink is a friendly color so, if used with care, it is an excellent choice for living rooms.

ORANGE: This is the color of confidence, of joy, and sociability—so what could be better for a living room? It stimulates joyfulness, release of emotions, and is the ideal backdrop for a party. It doesn't need to be hot orange, there are lots of tones. Think Etruscan vases and Italian frescoes—dusty, dusky, yellowy oranges.

YELLOW: The sunshine color lifts spirits, banishes depression, and raises energy

levels. It's a great choice for living rooms as it's brilliant for boosting self-esteem and makes you feel sociable and friendly. It looks fabulous with soft, creamy colors and is good friends with blue too.

GREEN: Green sits exactly in the middle of the color spectrum. Our eyes don't have to adjust to it, so it is exceedingly calming and reassuring. It's not a popular choice for living rooms but I have to say I love it and return to it again and again. It's a really good choice if your living room has to double up as a study or even a bedroom. I love to mix it with vibrant red and warm wood, but it

also looks lovely with dusky pinks and soft apricots.

BLUE: Blue can work in a living room but you will need to be clever. It's a cool color so very relaxing, but it can look and feel a little too cold. However, there are soft, warmer blues which can look stunning. Blue also teams up beautifully with warm brown tones for a distinctive modern look.

VIOLET AND MAUVE: These are soothing, meditative colors which are often used for bedrooms and meditation spaces. However, if you carry it off, lilac,

lavender, and foxglove tones can give a fresh take on living rooms (particularly when teamed with fresh white and cream). They also make an unusual accent color for furnishings.

WHITE: White is clean and calming but it can be very stark. However, there is white and white—many people find a combination of white and cream tones make for a serene, uncluttered feel. Of course you can always use white tones as a backdrop and then run wild (or restrained) with colored accessories. This looks wonderful and is very adaptable.

Clever ways with color

You don't have to paint the entire room—here are some other thoughts on how to use color in the living room:

- Play with colored glass. Suspend stained glass panels in your windows—or paint jars and bottles (glass paint is available from art stores) and display against the light.
- Hang multifaceted crystals in the window and watch the rainbows dance around the room (children and animals adore them).
- Buy junk furniture and experiment with paint colors and finishes.
- Relearn papier-mâché and construct distinctive bowls, platters, and dishes. Alternatively, make structures out of chicken wire and papier-mâché over the top.

- Go wild with flowers—choose bold arrangements of one color or stir it all up with a clashing cacophony of shades. Make a pact with yourself to try different flowers from your usual favorites.
- If you're bored of all your vases, try painting them, mosaic-ing them, or gilding them (check out art stores for wild ideas).
- Color your lighting. Aside from interesting shades, experiment with different colored light bulbs.

Scent

Often we notice the smell of a room before we even register how it looks. Whether it's the delicious scent of roses

or the stale pong of unwashed socks, our noses are incredibly delicate. However, please try to steer clear of synthetic fragrances and odor eliminators. They are often packed with nasty chemicals and only serve to mask smells.

The first rule is to keep rooms scrupulously clean and fresh. We don't actually need all those chemical cleaners—simple beeswax is ideal for wood furniture (and smells divine); add a few drops of essential oil to your feather duster and everything will smell gorgeous.

Flowers bring their own subtle smell. Don't limit them to vases—try growing scented flowers just outside your living room (so the scent will waft through open windows) or in window boxes.

Aromatherapy is *the* smell-good tool for your living room. If you want to introduce a particular mood then this is the easiest, swiftest way to do so. Scented candles are subtle and lovely but make sure they use pure oils and not synthetic perfumes. The space-clearing sprays I've already mentioned smell good, while purifying your space. Alternatively, make your own mist spray by filling a house-plant mister with purified water and then adding around fifteen drops of oil. Shake and then use— you'll find it's much nicer than aerosol air fresheners. The other tried and trusted method is to use an aromatherapy burner or diffuser in which a tea light warms a reservoir of water into which you add a few drops of your favorite oil. Make sure you remember to keep the water topped up or you'll end up with a ghastly goo.

The oils you choose are up to you but here are some ideas, with oils grouped according to the mood they tend to induce.

RELAXING: camomile, neroli, rose, lavender, jasmine

CALMING: geranium, lavender, melissa, ylang ylang

UPLIFTING: bergamot, hyssop, orange, yarrow

ENERGIZING: orange, peppermint, pine, rosemary, juniper, grapefruit

FUN-LOVING (ideal for parties): coriander, juniper, mandarin, tuberose

Be wary about buying room blends "off the shelf," as many "aromatherapy" products aren't pure. Check the ingredients carefully and make sure they only contain pure essential oils (a carrier oil such as sweet almond is fine). My favorite blends of the moment are those of the very talented aromatherapist Michelle Roques-O'Neil (see "Resources"). Her burning essences are masterful blends guaranteed to provide the ambience you want. I love Cocoon (deeply calming and protecting), Inspiration (reviving and restoring), and Rapture (warm and sensual). Alternatively, you could ask your local professional aromatherapist to put together a tailor-made blend for your home.

Sound

Try to spend a day becoming aware of the sounds within your living room (and your home in general)—it can be a real ear-opener. Often we're quite unaware of the sound or level of noise (or lack of it) which surrounds us. It's only once you become aware of your own noises that you can decide if you like them or not. Some people find they are actually uncomfortable with a lack of noise—they like the sound of neighbors and the bustle of the street, and feel lost without

it. Others simply crave silence or at least relative peace. There's no right or wrong answer to this—only individual preferences. But remember that sound has the power to heal and also to harm. It can soothe and calm, energize and uplift, but it also has the ability to irritate the nerves and make us feel tense and jittery. So choose the sounds with which you surround yourself with care.

Let's think about how you might play with sound in your living room.

- Allow the sounds outside to enter by throwing open windows. Alternatively, if you can't abide the noise outside or from next door, it may be worth investing in double glazing or sound-proofing.

- Make your own music. Do you play an instrument? Did you learn one as a child? Would you like to learn to play now? Do you have friends who are handy with a guitar or mandolin?

- Drumming echoes our heartbeat and can be very grounding and calming. Anyone can tap out a rhythm—practice and you could become expert.
- Experiment with different music styles and see how they make you feel. Don't dismiss anything until you have truly listened to it.
- Nature's sounds can be very soothing—particularly if you live in a busy urban neighborhood. You can buy recordings of birdsong, dolphins, whales, waterfalls, and the sound of the sea— all of which can be lovely.
- Introduce natural sounds as well— wind chimes, waterfalls, and bubbling water features are great feng shui and can be soothing (or irritating, so be aware of your own responses to them).
- Play with silence. Do you always have music on, or the radio or television? If so, spend time without these external noises and see how you feel.

The Creative Living Room

As we've already discovered, the living room is the most public room in the home. It's the place where you entertain guests, where you allow the outside world a glimpse of your private, personal self. Maybe this is why so many people plump for somewhat "proper" living rooms, decorated tastefully and "in fashion," adorned with "nice" ornaments and pictures. Obviously, if you want to keep your psyche tucked away, if you dislike the idea of others gaining a glimpse of your soul, then fine, keep it that way. But remember, you have to live here too. If we furnish a home with objects that reflect our inner being, we stand on the threshold of great discoveries.

Images and objects are powerful; they speak directly to the soul and can bring up intense emotions. Maybe this is another reason why it's often easier and safer to surround ourselves with anodyne, homogenous things.

"Soul" objects are like a wake-up call to the psyche; every time you pass them, they give you a kind of jolt, fresh insights, old memories, new directions. They also provide a great talking point when you do have people in your home.

I always beg people to think and feel deeply about the objects and images with which they furnish their homes—and particularly their living rooms. The one thing that fills me with horror is watching people browse around huge interiors stores buying up "finishing touches" en masse for a room: a handful of banal prints, a couple of vases, a "witty" (how I loathe that word) ornament or two. Sure, they will fill a gap, perhaps provide a bit of color, but what do they do for the soul?

I would urge you to take time to find art and objects imagined by human hearts and lovingly brought into creation by human hands, rather than simply buying up mass-produced things. These "soul" items do not have to cost the earth. Often they are far cheaper than the flashy, showy fashion "objets" that fill the interior-design magazines. They are not things to be bought on a purposeful shopping trip. It's just not possible to go out with a shopping list of "soul things"—they are items to be discovered, or purchased, over a lifetime, slowly, softly, with care and wonder.

Soul searching

Take a good hard look around your living room. What images do you have on the wall? What do they say to you? Do they still have meaning or has their time been and gone? Remember that our needs shift and change over the years. Much as I loved my pre-Raphaelite posters as a student, I'm not sure I'd want them around me now. What ornaments and objects have been in residence for years? Do you like them? Many of us keep things on show because we were given them or feel they were too expensive to

get rid of. Often we simply don't even think about what items we live with—they are simply "part of the furniture." Perhaps it's time to reconsider. If they are only so much outworn clutter then either sell them, give them to family or friends, or donate them to a charity shop. Don't feel guilty—it's time to move on.

Then, slowly, carefully, keep your eye open for things that really "talk" to you. I can't tell you what they will be—it's a "you" thing. However, if you're really stuck, here are a few pointers:

- Look to nature. What could be more beautiful than a piece of driftwood, a wonderful stone, a discarded antler?
- Discover your inner artist and make your own things. Take up a pottery, painting, basket-weaving, tapestry, or rag-rugging class—whatever appeals. If classes aren't your thing, go it alone. Try using unusual materials: baskets woven from local twigs and moss; rag rugs fashioned from recycled plastic; collages made from interesting bits of rubbish. Frame your own pictures or

those of your children. Be proud of your achievements.

- Look to native cultures that are still in touch with their souls and that possess a sense of true craft. Many galleries and stores now import beautiful items; or go shopping on your travels (but be wise though—many items which look wonderful in their native setting don't translate so well to Western interiors).

- Hunt out your own local craftspeople—they may be producing just what you

crave right on your doorstep. Many will happily work with you to bring your own vision to reality.

- When you go traveling, make a point of checking out local craft guilds—many towns also have "craft trails" and maps.

- Patronize student graduation shows. Many young artists and craftspeople have a freshness and spontaneity to their work that can be quite mind-blowing. I have bought several of my favorite things this way. There is also the piquant thought that you might be buying the work of a famous artist of the future.

- Always have at least some books in your living room, both for your own enjoyment and to interest your guests. Be aware, however, that there is nothing more telling than a person's choice of reading matter.

The natural living room

One of the nicest ways of bringing a sense of warmth and life to a living room is to look to nature. In particular, try to represent each of the elements in some way to give balance and harmony to your space. Bringing nature into your home means surrounding yourself with the healing and blessing of the outside world. We so often forget that we are part of that world—bringing in small reminders can be immensely healing.

WOOD: Wood is a living, breathing entity with a myriad colors, scents, and textures. Most tribal peoples believe that each tree has its own soul or spirit—so wood is a powerful ally if chosen with care and treated with respect. We've already talked about wooden floors and paneling, and beautiful wooden furniture such as chairs, tables, coffee tables,

sideboards, and shelves. Wood also makes marvelous candlesticks—and there is nothing more pleasing than a cleverly turned wooden bowl or platter. Baskets made from local materials such as withies, rushes, twigs, and hemp make useful receptacles for papers, wood, toys, and craft materials.

EARTH: Ceramics come in endless forms—from highly refined porcelain to rough earthenware; from delicate tiny figurines to monumental urns and figures. Then there is stone itself. I like to use large stones as doorstops and also have several small cairns around the home. They give a pausing point and are always a huge hit with small children and babies.

Crystals are the earth's treasure chest uncovered, a dragon's hoard you can

quietly bring into your home. There is a whole healing art devoted to crystals (see "Further Reading" for some introductory books) but, even if you're not convinced by those claims, they look wonderful, which is cause enough to buy some. I love the idea of having a guardian crystal for each room. You should pick one that "speaks" to you—but here are some ideas for stones that work well in living rooms:

- Citrine: Clears your thoughts and gives confidence and optimism. It is said to encourage friendship and dispel fear. Citrine is also supposed to help you accumulate or retain abundance.

- Jade: A popular stone said to increase vitality. It is a protective stone that will help heal and harmonize your space. It is also supposed to help prolong life and put things in perspective.

- Rock Crystal (quartz): A versatile crystal that balances and amplifies energy. You can easily project your own desires and needs for your living room onto it and the stone will help you achieve your purpose.

- Rose Quartz: A soft, gentle stone said to promote peace and self-esteem. It is useful if the energy in your living room tends to be disruptive and argumentative. Rose quartz supports children and families in particular.

- Turquoise: Protecting and strengthening, turquoise is said to promote strength, success, fulfillment, and a strong sense of spirit. It encourages clear communication, good relationships, and greater self-awareness, so it's an ideal stone for the living room.

Once you have chosen your crystal, you will need to cleanse it (crystals easily pick up other people's energy). Simply mix together one cup of spring water and half a cup of sea salt (ordinary table salt will do if you don't have sea salt). Plunge your crystal into the mixture and leave for at least twenty-four hours (some people like to leave the mixture in the sunlight but it's not essential). You can now dedicate your crystal to the energy you would like in your living room. Simply hold it and focus your energy and intention into it.

Fire

If you can possibly have a living hearth in your room, do so. The hearth was always the heart and soul of any home—it provides a space for the sacred fire that keeps the very spirit of the home alive. A living room with a living fire at its source always has a special feeling. Fire brings energy to the home; it is warming, protecting, and nurturing. A fire burning in your living room hearth will provide a natural focus for a family get-together or for solitary musing.

Obviously, not every home can have an open fire but it's still a nice idea to have a fireplace, a hearth. In this you can group candles to symbolize the fire and provide a safe place for the fire element. I also tend to have candles all around my living room. For me, they are an essential part of the furnishing of my room—as important as the sofa. They are also a great way to ring the changes in your room. I find that in the summer months I tend to have lighter colored candles, often with sweet, flowery scents while, as winter draws near, my candles get darker and their scents become woodier and more sensual.

Water

Water soothes and calms the soul—
it is purifying and healing. If your home
lacks humidity, place beautiful bowls of
clean fresh water around your living
room. Try adding petals or flowers to
float on top, and sink beautiful pebbles,
shells, or colored glass nuggets to
the bottom. An aquarium of fish
enlivens the energy of the room as
we've seen in the feng shui chapter;
so too do waterfall features. Spray your
room with misters and air fresheners—
misting can neutralize unpleasant
emotional charges and introduce
healing negative ions.

Air

It's easy to forget about the element of air,
yet it can easily become stagnant and heavy
in a room. Throw open your windows every
day for at least five minutes (yes, even in
winter). Improve air quality by using an air
purifier—keep one by the television in
particular. And don't forget fans— they look
stylish and keep air moving in hot climates.

Incense and burning aromatherapy oils
are recommended by ancient cultures for
attracting the spirits of the air. Don't overdo
the incense though—it can provoke asthma
and breathing difficulties. It's better to keep
it for home rituals and ceremonies rather
than as a background scent.

A Room with Spirit

We've talked a lot about the living room as a social, lively space—but it also needs to nurture you when you want to be alone. Virtually every enlightened architect points out that the living room should not consist of large open spaces alone, but must include places of retreat; small hidden corners. I remember clearly as a child having a "special" place behind my grandmother's sofa. A tiny stool and a kind of tray-table furnished my private world. Here I retreated to read, draw, and make things; to muse and ponder. Although the adults were only a footstep away, I was alone yet not lonely; an ideal state of affairs. "Most of us have a favorite place," says David Pearson, architect and natural homes expert, "the old inglenook within a large fireplace... the rocking chair... a half-hidden window seat, secluded corners, nooks, and crannies..."

Ensure your living room has places for people to "hide away." If your room doesn't have any natural nooks and crannies, you might make your own by skillful placement of chairs and other furniture. You might want to install a

screen or simply a chair or two into which one can sink completely. Inviting areas need not be quite so obvious. A huge hairy rug or sheepskin can invite loungers. A squashy beanbag or piles of cushions (in touchy, feely fabrics) can make snug retreats. Large, thick curtains can drape over furniture to make magical dens for children.

Altars

One activity I seem to recommend in virtually every book I write is altar-building. It is such a simple thing to do yet it can bring an instant sense of spirit into any space. I think I like altars so much because in this crazy, hectic world they allow us to stop for a moment. They pull us into the present, they allow us a chance to pause, to take stock, to figure out who we are and what our true selves really need.

Altar-building is probably almost as old as humankind itself. Our Neolithic ancestors certainly kept certain places sacred and invested them with a numinous quality. In ancient Greece and Rome, altars were built in every house for the household gods (the lares and penates) and other deities. Many faiths still keep this tradition alive today.

However, an altar need not be a place of religious ritual—it's simply a place of spiritual focus, a small hearth for the spirit. You probably already have subconscious altars in your living room—a collection of "soul" objects, a grouping of beloved family photographs, perhaps. These are altars of the heart.

If you're not sure about how to furnish an altar, use the following basic formula as a guide. An altar traditionally contained things to represent the four elements plus other objects:

- Earth is honored using something living (a plant or flowers) or something made from the fabric of earth (a stone, bowl of earth or salt, a piece of wood perhaps).
- Air is represented by incense or aromatherapy oil burning (the smoke moves through the air toward heaven).
- Fire is obviously represented by candles.
- Water is evoked by a bowl of clear fresh water or something brought from the sea or a river or pond.
- You could add a favorite image (a mandala, goddess, saint, angel) or statue.
- Crystals are at home on most altars.
- Photographs or meaningful pictures can be used.
- Some people like to have special books—or to write out affirmations, spells, or special passages.

Living room rituals

Rituals are another favorite practice of mine. Again, they need not be complicated or overtly religious (although if you have a particular faith it is wonderful to use prayers or sacred words and call upon a particular godhead or allies). A simple ritual can totally transform the feeling in a room. There isn't space to go into too many of these (see "Further Reading" for books to help), but try out these two to get a feel for the work.

Cleansing ritual

I like to use this if there has been an argument in the room, or a meeting or get-together which has been less than happy. It clears the air (in all senses) and restores peace and tranquility.

1 Cleanse yourself by having a shower using a few drops of rosemary oil (not if you're pregnant). As you cleanse yourself ask for help in removing any negativity you may have contributed to the atmosphere—and any bad feelings you may still harbor.

2 Space cleanse your room thoroughly (see pages 28–33).

3 Stand or sit quietly in the center of the room and ask your higher self for any information that could help you resolve the problem. Send unconditional love to all concerned—even if you still sneakily feel they were in the wrong.

Imagine love pouring out from your heart center to the other people involved in the argument. Send forgiveness.

4 Now shift the energy of the room with sound. Take a drum and bang noisily all around the room. Next, take a party squeaker and blow it noisily around the room—it's hard to remain stony-faced with such a silly sound.

5 Finish by spraying the room with a plant mister containing spring water and a few drops of the appropriate Bach Flower remedy: Beech (for intolerance and a need to be right); Vine (for a general domineering attitude); Vervain (for those who are over enthusiastic and fanatical); Chicory (for a tendency towards selfishness and possessiveness)—or, if you aren't sure, Rescue Remedy.

Energizing ritual

This ritual is ideal for carrying out before a party or any gathering you want to be lively, fun, and enjoyable. It provides a welcoming, happy, jolly atmosphere—and gets you in the mood as well.

1 Cleanse yourself with a shower, adding a few drops of peppermint oil.

2 Space cleanse the room (see pages 28–33).

3 Light orange and yellow candles around the room (you may like to leave these in place for the party, in which case ensure they are in safe places).

4 Burn some essential oils—grapefruit, lemon, orange, or geranium are good lively choices.

5 Put on some music with a strong rhythm (something with a good earthy base line or decent drumming). Let your foot start tapping, feel your body start to respond to the music, and finally let yourself go and really dance. As you dance, imagine how it will be when other people are dancing with you—or enjoying lively, vivacious conversation.

6 If you have any spirit animals or guardian angels, ask them to bring joy and delight to your party.

7 You should feel your own energy start to shift. Continue dancing until you have heightened the energy to the level you desire.

8 Now imagine that energy concentrating in your solar plexus (abdominal area). It builds up into a ball of glittering, pulsing orange-red light. Imagine that ball bursting out and spreading to every corner of the room.

9 Stamp your feet to bring yourself back to reality. Have something to eat (and maybe to drink) and enjoy your party.

Farewell and be happy

This small book is now at an end. I do
hope it has prompted you to look at your
living room in a fresh way. Don't expect
to shift your entire living room in one fell
swoop—creating a spiritful space is an
organic process, an exploration, a
journey. I wish you years of happiness in
your own living space: joyful gatherings,
peaceful solitary moments, laughter and
thoughtfulness. Above all, remember that
the key to a living room lies in its name.
Whatever life choices you make, don't be
scared to live life to the full. Experience
everything (both good and bad) to the
utmost. Your living room should always
await you—a soothing, nurturing, safe
space in which to sift through your
experiences, both in company and alone.

Resources

Michelle Roques-O'Neil's aromatherapy products can be mail ordered from her website **www.aromaroquesoneil.com**

Precious Earth is a wonderful source of environmentally friendly and ecologically sensitive building and decorating products. Check them out for eco paints, wallpapers, flooring, and lighting—as well as plasters, renders, and woodland products. **www.preciousearth.co.uk**

Natural Building Technologies (**www.natural-building.co.uk**) are also great for natural paints, oils, and waxes.

My website **www.smudging.com** has lots of information on all aspects of holistic living. You can also buy my other books on-line and get in touch with me via the site.

The following websites supply space-clearing sprays:
Pacific Essences **www.pacificessences.com**
Australian Bush Flower Essences
  www.ausflowers.com.au
Alaskan Essences **www.alaskanessences.com**

Further reading

- *Spirit of the Home* (Watson-Guptill) was my first book on holistic living and provides more detail on many of the topics in this book. You may also be interested in the companion books in this series: *Spirit of the Bedroom, Spirit of the Kitchen,* and *Spirit of the Nursery* (all Watson-Guptill).
- *House as a Mirror of Self* by Clare Cooper Marcus is essential reading for anyone interested in how we relate to our homes.
- *Heart & Home* by Beverly Pagram is a lovely book, packed with soulful ideas (and lovely pictures) to inspire every room in the house, not just the living room. Her other books, *Heaven & Hearth* and *Natural Housekeeping* are also well worth reading.
- For more on space clearing and rituals for the home, check out my earlier books, *Sacred Rituals at Home, The Smudge Pack,* and *The Energy Secret.* I'm also a big fan of *Space Clearing* by Denise Linn and *Creating Sacred Space with Feng Shui* by Karen Kingston.
- For advice on altars read *Altars* by Denise Linn and *Altars Made Easy* by Peg Streep.

• For more on feng shui read *Interior Design with Feng Shui* by Sarah Rossbach, *Feng Shui Made Easy* by William Spear, *Feng Shui for Your Home* by Sarah Shurety and *The Feng Shui House Book* by Gina Lazenby (Watson-Guptill).

Picture Credits

Crown Paints: vi, 59 (right)
The Cotswold Company: 65
Ducal Ltd/Graham Henderson: 56
Elizabeth Whiting Associates: 11, 13 (middle), 14, 42, 47, 49, 51, 66, 69, 71, 81
Fired Earth: 8, 19
The Holding Company: 27 (left), 27 (middle), 63
ICI Paints/Dulux: 58 (left), 58 (right), 59 (left)
The Interior Archive/Andrew Wood: 34, 85
Laura Ashley Ltd: 24, 41 (middle), 74, 79, 83, 88
McCord: 18 (left), 18 (right), 27 (right), 39

New England Lifestyle: 13 (left)
OKA: 4, 41 (left)
Red Cover: (Adrian Wilson) 77; (Andreas von Einsiedel) 3, 44; (Brian Harrison) 29, 86; Graham Atkins-Hughes) 22; (James Merrell) 73; (Mark York) 61; (Winfried Heinze) 6
Robert Harding: 13 (right), 17, 21, 70
Sofa Workshop Direct: 53
Tom Faulkner/Anthony Cowell and Neil Mason: 26, 41 (right)
Andy Whale/FPG International/Getty Images: 31